The Little Book of British Butterflies

PAUL DUFFIELD

CONTENTS

INTRODUCTION

This book is a pocket reference guide to the species of butterflies that are found in Britain.

Colour illustrations are provided together with brief information about distribution and habitat of each species.

The little book of British butterflies is one of a series of small reference guides designed to take up very little room in a pocket or backpack, but still provide enough information to identify the flora and fauna of Britain.

This book is also available for the Amazon Kindle and other electronic readers such as tablets and mobile phones using the Amazon Kindle app.

FAMILY HESPERIIDAE (SKIPPERS)

Hesperiidae, known as Skippers, are small butterflies with short plump bodies and hooked antennae. Most are primarily orange or brown in colour.

CHEQUERED SKIPPER
Carterocephalus palaemon

Inhabits grassland on the edges of open broadleaf woodland. It has been extinct in England since the mid 1970s but is still found in western Scotland.

DINGY SKIPPER
Erynnis tages

Inhabits woodland clearings, coastal dunes, and chalk downs. While distribution is patchy it is found throughout Britain.

ESSEX SKIPPER
Thymelicus lineola

Inhabits dry grassland in open sunny areas, roadside verges, woodlands and coastal marshland. It is widely distributed in central and southern England.

GRIZZLED SKIPPER
Pyrgus malvae

Inhabits wood clearings, chalk downland and scrub grassland. It is found throughout southern and central England and Wales, but has declined in several areas.

LARGE SKIPPER
Ochlodes sylvanus

Inhabits hedgerows, woodland clearings and areas of tall grassland. It is present in England, Wales and south west Scotland.

LULWORTH SKIPPER
Thymelicus acteon

Inhabits sheltered or south facing slopes of chalk downland and coastal grassland. It is mainly restricted to the south Dorset coast.

SILVER-SPOTTED SKIPPER
Hesperia comma

Inhabits areas of chalk downland. Although once common it is now only present in southern England, mainly found in Dorset, Hampshire and Wiltshire.

SMALL SKIPPER
Thymelicus sylvestris

Inhabits open areas of rough grassland, road verges, edges of fields and woodlands. It is widely distributed in Britain up to North Yorkshire and the border of Scotland.

FAMILY: PAPILIONIDAE (SWALLOWTAILS)

Papilionidae, known as swallowtails are large colourful butterflies. Only one species of papilionidae is found in Britain.

SWALLOWTAIL
Papilio machaon

Inhabits areas of fen vegetation in the Norfolk Broads. Rarely, but occasionally, seen in other parts of Britain.

FAMILY: PIERIDAE (WHITES)

Pieridae, known as whites are mostly white, yellow or orange in coloration, often displaying black spots.

BATH WHITE
Pontia daplidice

A rare vistor to Britain very few specimens have been recorded since the early 20th century. The few recent sightings in recent year have been on the south coast of Dorset.

BRIMSTONE
Gonepteryx rhamni

Inhabits scrubby grassland and woodland and is often seen near hedgerows and roadside verges. It is found throughout central and southern England and parts of Ireland.

CLOUDED YELLOW
Colias croceus

Inhabits flowered areas, especially unimproved chalk downlands. It is widely distributed in Britain and especially common near the coasts of southern England.

GREEN-VEINED WHITE
Pieris napi

Inhabits damp areas of vegetation im meadows, moorland, woods and near lakes, rivers and ponds. It is widespread throughout Britain.

LARGE WHITE
Pieris brassicae

Inhabits a wide range of areas, especially allotments and gardens where cabbages are cultivated. It is widespread throughout Britain.

ORANGE-TIP
Anthocharis cardamines

Inhabits damp areas of woodland glades, hedgerows, meadows and the banks of streams and rivers. It is widespread throughout Britan.

PALE CLOUDED YELLOW
Colias hyale

A rare vistor to Britain very few specimens have been recorded since the early 20th century. Specimens are occasionally sighted in the south of England and Ireland.

SMALL WHITE
Pieris rapae

Inhabits a wide range of areas, especially allotments and gardens where cabbages are cultivated. It is widespread throughout Britain.

WOOD WHITE
Leptidea sinapis

Inhabits areas of grassland in woodland clearings and some coastal cliffs. It is found in central and southern England and parts of Ireland.

FAMILY: LYCAENIDAE (HAIRSTREAKS, COPPERS AND BLUES)

Lycaenidae, known as hairstreaks, coppers and blues are small and brightly coloured, some species having a metallic sheen.

ADONIS BLUE
Lysandra bellargus

Inhabits south facing slopes in grassland areas of chalk or limestone. It is found in Dorset, Wiltshire, Sussex and Kent.

BLACK HAIRSTREAK
Satyrium pruni

Inhabits woodland glades and hedgerows in areas densely populated with Blackthorn. It is rare and only found in Oxfordshire and Cambridgeshire.

BROWN ARGUS
Aricia agestis

Inhabits areas of chalk and limestone grassland, coastal dunes, heathland and woodland clearings. It is widespread in central and southern England and the coast of Wales.

BROWN HAIRSTREAK
Thecla betulae

Inhabits areas of blackthorn hedges, scrub and edges of woodland. Mostly found in south west Wales, Surrey, Sussex, Devon and Cornwall.

CHALKHILL BLUE
Lysandra coridon

Inhabits limestone and chalk grassland areas. Mostly found in southern England.

COMMON BLUE
Polyommatus icarus

Inhabits coastal dunes, road verges, woodland clearings, areas of waste ground and open uncultivated areas such as disused quarries. Widespread throughout Britan.

DUKE OF BURGUNDY
Hamearis lucina

Inhabits limestone and chalk grassland areas and woodland clearings. Mostly found in central southern England but small populations exist in other areas.

GREEN HAIRSTREAK
Callophrys rubi

Inhabits areas of chalk grassland, woodland clearings, heaths, moors and boggy areas. Widespread thoughout Britan.

HOLLY BLUE
Celastrina argiolus

Inhabits hedgerows and woodlands as well as urgan areas such as parks and gardens. Widespread in England and Wales with some populations in Ireland and Scotland.

LARGE BLUE
Maculinea arion

Inhabits coastal and limestone grassland areas. Very rare in Britain, currently found only in south west England where it has been reintroduced by conservation groups.

NORTHERN BROWN ARGUS
Aricia artaxerxes

Inhabits grassland areas of sand dunes, coastal valleys and quarries. Found in Scotland and northern counties of England.

PURPLE HAIRSTREAK
Neozephyrus quercus

Inhabits woodlands, hedgerows and areas of parkland. Widespread in England and Wales with some populations in Scotland and Ireland.

SILVER-STUDDED BLUE
Plebejus argus

Inhabits areas of chalk and limestone grassland, heaths and sand dunes. Found in North Wales and counties of southern England.

SMALL BLUE
Cupido minimus

Inhabits chalk and limestone grassland, dunes, quarries and embankments. Mainly found in south central England with some populations on the coasts of Ireland and Scotland.

SMALL COPPER
Lycaena phlaeas

Inhabits chlk grassland, woodland clearings, heaths, waste ground and moorland. Widespread throughout Britain except uplands of northern Britain.

WHITE-LETTER HAIRSTREAK
Satyrium w-album

Inhabits hedgerows, woodlands and areas of mixed scrub. Widespread in England and Wales but less common in far western areas.

FAMILY: NYMPHALIDAE (ARISTROCRATS, FRITILLARIES AND BROWNS)

Nymphalidae, known as aristocrats, fritillaries and browns are medium to large sized butterflies, many of which are brightly coloured.

COMMA
Polygonia c-album

Inhabits edges and open areas of woodland and often seen in gardens. Widespread in England and Wales, some populations also found in Scotland and Ireland.

DARK GREEN FRITILLARY
Argynnis aglaja

Inhabits limestone and chalk grassland, coastal dunes, moorlands and woodland clearings. Found throughout Britain but less common in eastern areas.

GATEKEEPER
Pyronia tithonus

Inhabits hedgerows, woodlands and heaths. Found in southern counties of England, Wales and the far south of Ireland.

GLANVILLE FRITILLARY
Melitaea cinxia

Inhabits coastal grassland, areas of chalk downland and woodland clearings. Populations are restricted to the Isle of Wight.

GRAYLING
Hipparchia semele

Inhabits chalk grassland, woodlands, dry areas of heaths, disused quarries and derelict industrial sites. Found throughout Britain mainly in coastal areas.

HEATH FRITILLARY
Melitaea athalia

Inhabits woodlands and heathland valleys. A rare endangered species found only in areas of Cornwall, Devon, Essex and Kent.

HIGH BROWN FRITILLARY
Argynnis adippe

Inhabits areas of grass and bracken and rocky limestone outcrops. A highly endangered species found in very few areas of England and Wales.

LARGE HEATH
Coenonympha tullia

Inhabits wet areas of heathland, moorland and bogs. Found in northern Britain and throughlout Ireland.

MARBLED WHITE
Melanargia galathea

Inhabits areas of chalk and limestone grassland, coastal grassland, woodland clearings, verges and embankments. Found in southern and central England and south Wales.

MARSH FRITILLARY
Euphydryas aurinia

Inhabits damp areas of grassland and woodland clearings. Found in south west and central southern England, western areas of Wales and Scotland and Northern Ireland.

MEADOW BROWN
Maniola jurtina

Inhabits coastal dunes, heaths, hay meadows, hedgerows, road verges and woodland clearings. Found throughout Britain.

19

MOUNTAIN RINGLET
Erebia epiphron

Inhabits damp areas of mountain grassland. Populations are restricted to mountain areas of central Scotland and the Lake District.

PAINTED LADY
Vanessa cardui

Inhabits dry open areas and often seen in in large numbers in cultivated flowery areas of parks and gardens. Widespread throughout Britain.

PEACOCK
Inachis io

Inhabits a wide range of habitats and often seen in cultivated areas of parks and gardens. Found throughout Britain.

PEARL-BORDERED FRITILLARY
Boloria euphrosyne

Inhabits areas of bracken and grass and woodland clearings. Widespread in northern Scotland, Cumbria, Devon, Cornwall and south east England.

PURPLE EMPEROR
Apatura iris

Inhabits areas of broadleaved woodland and Willow. Widespread in England and Wales with populations in areas of Scotland and Ireland.

RED ADMIRAL
Vanessa atalanta

Inhabits a wide range of areas including gardens, coastal areas, towns and villages towns. Common throughout Britain.

RINGLET
Aphantopus hyperantus

Inhabits areas of damp grassland, verges, riverbanks and woodland clearings. Found throughout Britain except northern Scotland.

SCOTCH ARGUS
Erebia aethiops

Inhabits limestone grassland, woodland clearings and boggy areas. Widespread in Scotland, some populations exist in areas of England.

SILVER-WASHED FRITILLARY
Argynnis paphia

Inhabits areas of broadleved and mixed woodland and hedgerows. Found in southern England and Wales and throughout Ireland.

SMALL HEATH
Coenonympha pamphilus

Inhabits areas of dry, well drained grassland, woodland clearings, coastal dunes and road verges. Found throughout Britain.

SMALL PEARL-BORDERED FRITILLARY
Boloria selene

Inhabits areas of damp grassland, moorland, wood pasture and woodland clearings. Mainly found in western areas of Britain.

SMALL TORTOISESHELL
Aglais urticae

Inhabits a wide range of areas, often seen in cultivated flowery areas of parks and gardens. Found throughout Britain.

SPECKLED WOOD
Pararge aegeria

Inhabits woodland clearings, hedgerows, parks and gardens. Found throughout all but far northern areas of England, Wales, Ireland and northern Scotland.

WALL
Lasiommata megera

Inhabits areas of short grassland, coastal dunes, disused quarries, embankments and gardens. Widespread in England, Wales and Ireland.

WHITE ADMIRAL
Limenitis camilla

Inhabits shaded areas of mature deciduous and mixed woodland. Restricted to areas of southern and central England.

ACKNOWLEDGMENTS

Images adapted from illustrations by Edmund Evans from 'Coleman's British Butterflies', 1895, Rev. Francis Orpen Morris from 'A History of British Butterflies', 1852 and James Duncan from 'Natural History of British Butterflies', 1840.

ABOUT THE AUTHOR

Paul Duffield is an author with a keen interest in the countryside.

He became interested in nature at a young age and having lived, worked, fished and walked over many parts of Britain he realised that a series of small easy to carry reference books on fish, plants, birds, insects and other animals would be ideal for anyone with an interest in the natural world.

Printed in Great Britain
by Amazon